DOGGEREL
& WORSE

DOGGEREL
& WORSE
by Elly Robinson

To Bruce

ISBN 978-0-9926877-3-1

Jardine Press 2014

text & cover design © Elly Robinson

Doggerel

What could be merrier than a wire-haired fox terrier?
(Apart from a glass of champagne)
There's nothing so sweet as those four furry feet
Except when they've been in the rain –
She makes doggy prints on my nice flowery chintz
So? I'll just do that washing again!

She's my most faithful friend – loves me without end
Without her – where would I be?
I could spend summer days on sun-kissed holidays
Blue skies, silver sand sparkling sea –
I could stay out all night, catch a show, drinks and a bite
If she wasn't waiting at home for me

 I'd go to lectures and talks instead of long walks
Wouldn't play in the park with a ball
I'd see every movie while dressed up so groovy
No more muddy boots in my hall!
And when I got home, I'd be all alone!
That would be no fun at all

CONTENTS

INTRODUCTION

My sister's name is Elly May Bags, at least that's what I've always called her. Our parents had named her Elaine Margaret, but she despised E-Lane and later Margaret more, hence Elly May Bags for as long as I can remember. We didn't have a happy childhood. There was no money and a constant stench of divorce. One of my earliest memories is sitting with Elly May Bags at the top of carpetless stairs, listening to rows and tears in the empty rooms below. We had some chairs. Then the next memory up is a recurring nightmare. We are three feet tall with our parents on the Clifton Suspension Bridge, just outside Bristol. Three hundred feet below is a great river full of drowning. I later understood that it was called the River Severn. One of the adults, a man wearing a trilby and evidently an associate of my parents, picked up Elly May Bags and held her over the side of the parapet. Such a gesture initiated much amusement amongst the grown-ups, my mother wittering in communal mirth. I stared at them in alarm. I was four years old and apparently the only person there who was horrified. I've never seen fear like I saw in my sister's face. Sixty years later and it's still on the night-time slate. Except this was no dream, it happened. We didn't know we were unhappy as kids because we had no one to compare love with. It was an age of lino round the edges with no carpet to cover the boards in between. In winter we dressed in the kitchen with the oven door open and never had a fire until our grandmother supplied thirty seven shillings and sixpence for a few sacks of coal. In 1951 the tortoise died of hypothermia. Elly May Bags and I were already more angry than we knew. I expressed it with asthma and she escaped with art. She drew things all the time. Mainly doggies. I passed my art exam at school in 1961 because she drew a transistor radio for me and everyone thought I had talent. I suppose it was one of the first great fraudulences of my life. But Elly May Bags' talent was real. She was accepted at St. Martin's School of Art and I started writing poems. I can still smell ink in the ribbon of a clapped-out Olivetti my grandfather had given me. But I was never any good at poems. She got a boyfriend I called "the Tottenham Hammer Yob" and our lives went their separate ways. I love Elly May Bags. Over half a century has passed and I'm proud of her doing what I could not. To my surprise she's written poems, and the reason I think they're good is because they're honest, and funny, and angry; valuable, because she nearly got thrown off a bridge..

B.R. September 2014
Bruce Robinson, creator of "Withnail & I"

WALKING

My Old Boots

These boots weren't made for talking
But when they smile with gaping lips
I stick them up with Araldite
And clamp their mouths with bulldog clips

My guardian angels with stout soles
And cherry blossom smiling faces
Carry me over hazards and holes
Hold me tight with your long laces

Carelessly kicked across the floor
Faithful friends full of the ghost of me
Wrinkled and waiting by the door
Always want to walk with me

Beachcombing

I walk on the wild windy beach alone
In search of the treasures that shine on the shore
Frosted sea glass, pearly shell, perfect stone

Here is a top shell – a rare spinning cone
Rosy pink spiral, rainbows in its core
I walk on the wild windy beach alone

But over the waves and the wild wind's moan
A young voice asks me what I'm looking for
Frosted sea glass, pearly shell, perfect stone

"I can't find no shark's teeth" he says with a groan
"I found a load here when I looked before"
I prefer the wild windy beach alone

"My little snake needs a bed of his own!"
I have no desire to hear any more
Frosted sea glass, pearly shell, perfect stone

I'm saved by the ring of his mobile phone
I don't want to see his boa constrictor
I walk on the wild windy beach alone
Frosted sea glass, pearly shell, perfect stone

The End of the Line

This old railway track where wildflowers now bloom
Was once a long life line to Brightlingsea
It's a waterside garden of roses and broom
And oak trees reflecting the sparkling sea

On a path of soft leaf mould, like chocolate fudge
I emerge from the tunnel of trees to the light
A breath of sea air blows over saltmarsh and sludge
Skimming scurvy grass, thrift and seablight

Beyond the low border of bramble and briar
Silent, white and determined
A little egret struggles higher and higher
And sails away on the west wind

Here by the creek is a miniature beach
Fringed with the pink fronds of tamarisk trees
And out in the mudflats just beyond reach
A skeleton ship no one else sees

I'm making my way to the old railway bridge
Though little of it remains
But a rusty tin shack by a crumbling ridge
And no tangible trace of the trains

One Morning in May

Distant calls of a cuckoo echo over the Stour
Cow parsley, horse chestnut, hawthorn in white flower
Rust red cattle graze in the lazy meadow
Swallows swoop over swans with soft cygnets in tow
Golden buttercup meadows bask in bliss
Is there nowhere on earth more lovely than this?
I walk through blue speedwell, pink campion, storksbill
Lilac trees scent the breeze – all is harmony – till
A vast metal monster unfolds its wide wings
From which a toxic cocktail of chemicals springs
A baying spraying preying metal mantis set free
To poison plants and to threaten and upset me
Now wild flowers are distorted, deformed and bent
And in the air – a miasma of venomous scent

Purple Fever

I had to go down to the woods again, on a wet and windy day
To sail on a sea of bluebells and see the squirrels play
Their chitter chatter like crackers maracas backing a blackbird's song
A chiff-chaff strummed while the wild wind hummed and moaned and droned along

The brisk breeze blew the woodland waves more violet than any blue
When close beside me appeared someone with hair of identical hue
Was this the wicked witch of the woods whose blue rinse had gone bad?
With a purple tsunami of hair like that – this person must surely be mad

I fled from the lavender lady till I could run no more
Feet crushing crispy cornflake leaves on the chestnut woodland floor
An abandoned engine seemed to float in the rustling rusty sea
And clinging to the wreckage grew soft mossy greenery

I was glad to get out of the woods again – although the wind was harsh
Blowing the blackthorn blossom on the scurvy grass of the marsh
Where a lonely little egret sailed, yellow socked, on the chilling blast
And a swan slithered over the salty silt while the tide was rising fast

A Sonnet for the Shipyard

Alkanet, blackberry bramble and broom
Coltsfoot, goosefoot, goose grass and germander
Dog rose, daisy, jack-go-to-bed-at-noon
Lizards and newts and the local dittander
Buddleia, buttercup, poor man's brush
Cow parsley, cow parsnip, jack by the hedge
Blackthorn and hawthorn, sharp flowered rush
Goatsbeard and hawksbeard and salt meadow sedge
Herb bennet, herb robert, poppy, plantain
Pink campion, white campion, ragwort, restharrow
Cranesbill and storksbill, thistle, fleabane
Kidney vetch, tufted vetch, toadflax and yarrow
Red clover, white clover and ribbed melilot
All gone now – developers levelled the lot

HEROES

Antony Gormley

I do think so warmly of Antony Gormley
He'd be a model dad
If I'd had the choice, I'd have chosen his voice
To tell me not to be bad

Imagine how the day'd go if he made all the play-dough
The fun would never end
He'd never be mean with his plasticine
He could literally make you a friend

Outside of the home, no garden gnome
Would ever go to waste
And with old compact discs he'd build bright obelisks
All in the best of taste

At home or away, any beach holiday
Would be beyond compare
All along the sand his figures would stand
Guarding castles in the air

Dylan Thomas the Tank Engine

Now Thomas was young and cheeky pulling coaches up Fern Hill
All along the sidings and happy as his boiler blue
His stumpy funnel coal black as night
Shunting on his six small wheels
Chuffing proudly as he puffed
Honoured among wagons he was the prince of the engine sheds
But oftentimes unkindly he would wake a big express
Whistling lewdly while it rested
And laughing loudly like a drain

Poetry in Motion

I'd like to be Rogered by Federer
He sets my poor heart aflame
I'd never swerve away from his serve
I'd be happy to play his love game

I'd love to be Rogered by Federer
I'd never challenge his calls
I wouldn't fret to be caught in his net
And would willingly hold his new balls

I'll never be Rogered by Federer
I'll never feel his naked bum
Or tear off his jacket, grab hold of his raquet
Coz I'm as old as his mum

Vincent

If I could whiz through time and space
And meet the great man face to face
I'd say: "Excuse me Mister Gogh –
Why did you cut your left ear off?

Did it resemble a cauliflower?
Or was it because it sapped your power?
And, next day in dawn's early light
Did you wish you'd chopped the right?

Why did that ear deserve such an end?
A peculiar present to send to a friend –
Let alone to give to an ungrateful tart
Who might have preferred a more suitable part

Yvonne

for Yvonne Skargon

She asked me to write how it felt to be her
Stuck there in a nursing home bed
All night and all day with nothing to do
Wishing that she was dead
To end her days in a place like that
Was something she used to dread
She wanted to be at home with her cats
And die in her own sweet bed

Not being able to draw or engrave
Must have been more than frustrating
Reading, remembering, waiting
Waiting for a visit from John
Waiting for a letter
Waiting for her glass of wine
Or maybe something better

I wanted to take her things that cheer
Pictures, books and flowers
To distract from those comfortless curtains
And brighten her waking hours
But words were all she asked of me
So I praised her to the skies
Now I can never look at a plant
Without seeing it through her eyes

LOVE

Blackheart Wolf

Blackheart wolf sniff round her door
She don't open it no more

Blackheart make her soft heart sing
She would give him everything
Blackheart sleep with her tonight
Blackheart slink off before daylight

Softheart bitch begin to cry
Every time he say goodbye
Softheart sad to be apart
To be without him break her heart

Blackheart dismiss her with a snort
Has a bitch in every port
Blackheart smile into the night
Forget her when she not in sight

Through the darkened streets he prowl
No one hear her silent howl
In misery she wait in pain
For Blackheart to come round again

Blackheart Wolf sniff round her door
She don't open it no more

Full of Fun

He's full of fun and flirty flattery
Emotional assault and battery
Breaking down my old defences
Destroying my protecting fences

Can't believe the way my head feels
My heart's turning crazy cartwheels
I'm teetering on the high wire
Afraid of falling in friendly fire

Head says NO! Heart says YES!
My moral fibre's in a mess
I'm falling and I'm willing to bet
There won't be any safety net

Heavenly Walk

On an Indian Summer's last golden day
We walk high on the hillside in heavenly light
On our path paved with acorns, golden leaves dance the way
Up high with the buzzards our spirits take flight
A garland of honour regales the hedgerow
Red fairy lights of holly, rosehips and haw
The blue blooms brightly on blackberry and sloe
As we gaze at each other like never before
I walked in the valley without you in spring
Through damp meadows of knapweed and clover
Near the pylons I heard the sweet nightingale sing
Yet was glad when the wet walk was over
Now the warm southerly wind blows our winters away
And the hope in our hearts is that's how it will stay

Lovesick Blues

You're sick of being lovesick
Bored stiff with being alone
Lying looking at the ceiling
Longing for him to phone

You're fed up with your feelings
He doesn't love you half enough
You know he'll be getting going
When the goings getting tough

You're pissed off by your passion
Depressed by your desire
He thinks love's gone out of fashion
While your poor heart's on fire

Love's a bittersweet addiction
When you're longing for a shot
Living in your private hell
And dreams are all you've got

Splitting

You start to notice little cracks
That never bothered you before
You're finding fault with everything
Don't want to be there anymore

Then, secretly, you play the field
Seeking a replacement
With itchy feet and roving eye
You contemplate displacement

And then at last you fall in love!
You can't hold back the tears
The house that you've been waiting for
For twenty million years

You take first steps to break away
You get a valuation
Hope someone will be glad to pay
For your discerning decoration

Yes! Someone wants to buy it!
With great relief you sigh
As you eagerly exchange contracts
A kind of house decree nisi

It's like a decree absolute
When you legally complete
And then at last the time has come
To steal away from soulless street

My Garden Angel

If you were an anagram, I'd be the answer
If you dabbled in drumming then I'd be your dancer
If you were a sculptor, you'd make me a statue
If you were a poodle I'd pamper and pat you
If you'd be the yang I yearn to be yin
I'm the five-lever lock and I'll let your key in

I'm a big fluffy ice cream frantic for your flake
Together a fine ninety-nine we could make
I'm your toasted brown bread – be my baked beans
I'd enjoy being a jumper if you were the jeans
I'm a slouchy soft sock – let me slip in your shoe
I could caress and give comfort to you

If I were a garden, you'd be a green tree
I'd be grateful and glad you were growing on me
I'd be a clematis clinging close to your holly
If black stormy clouds broke then I'd be your brolly
Whatever the weather, together we'd fly
I'd soar like a songbird with you in the sky

Wedding Sonnet
(with a nod to Shakespeare's Sonnet 116)

Let me not to the marriage of true hearts
Admit impediments. Loves merely shagging
Which falters every time the husband farts
Or wavers when the wife's accused of nagging;
She's housekeeper, counsellor, cleaner and cook.
She loves him deeply and forgives his sins
She picks up his socks while he's reading a book
Reluctant to ask him to take out the bins
Unfairly, he will get the better deal
At work or home – she labours just the same
Yet he always comes home to a gorgeous meal
While she gives up her freedom and her name.
It's wonderful to have someone to love you all your life
If only we women could have such a wife

FAMILY AND FRIENDS

Fear and Loathing in Puerto Rico
(From an email from my brother Bruce)

My family have all gone home
It's hot here and I'm all alone
With butterflies as big as books by day
Until the night falls. I'm convinced that they
Are creatures who just change their clothes
From lemonade lightness they metamorphose
To moths the size of bibles batting wings
And I'm afraid of these satanic things
I fear that they may bring my death.
My asthma's bad – can't catch my breath
I'm permanently feeling crappy
The film's as good as ever – so I'm happy
For someone who was born to be depressed.
My troubled soul will never let me rest

Little Angel

As an only child and a pretty one too
There was nothing on earth that she couldn't do
Today was her birthday – now she was seven
And the party at granny's was going to be heaven

She wore her brand new pink taffeta dress
Puff sleeved and full skirted; she felt like a princess
Everyone there, cousins uncles and aunts
asked the sweet birthday girl for a song and dance

This was the moment she'd been waiting for
She climbed on the table   higher up than the floor
She sang "A, you're adorable" waving her arms
Artistically dancing to "cuticle of charms"

Carrying on up to zed. Everyone started to clap
Her first taste of success! Uncle Bert gave her his cap
To go round them all and collect lots of money
She made quite a fortune! And felt famous and funny

She walked out of the party still glowing with pride
Dad waited impatient in the Austin outside
Inexplicably, this most mild mannered of men
Shouted red faced "Don't you ever do that again!"

It Happened in Wivenhoe

It happened in Wivenhoe – five years ago
When Nancy said: "Doris – I want you to know
There's someone I think you'll be certain to fancy;
If you're not meant for each other, then my name's not Nancy!"

It was just after Christmas two thousand and five
And before Doris' birthday – she'd be twentyfive
She was having a party – what a palaver!
She'd made copious cakes, which we'd wash down with Cava

"Now, Doris" said Nancy – "I'm telling you flat
You've got to ask me and invite my friend Matt
He's a bit of a brainbox but up for some fun
I want you to meet him – I just know he's The One!"

Several days in the kitchen chef Doris spent baking
Cakes of all sizes and shapes in the making
Invites were sent to the fortunate few
To act as the extras for the principal two

The house soon filled up with good friends, young and old
Though they sat by the fire, were kept out in the cold
By the radiant hostess; though looking her best
She only had eyes for the one honoured guest

I don't know what Nancy had promised young Matt
But he was rather interested – I'm quite sure of that
They gazed at each other and uttered no words
Stuck close to each other like peach-faced lovebirds

Together they sailed to another dimension
It was obvious what was their mutual intention
Everyone saw that their hearts were aglow
And Nancy said: "Elly, didn't I tell you so!"

Mourning in June

Nobody had told the weatherman that it was June
I'd woken from a dream of an angry dragon raging for my blood.
Heart pounding to the sound of wet branches whipping my window
as if I needed a reminder that this was the day of the funeral
Along the river and over the border the wind roars wilder
As I drive to the tragic gathering where I meet my daughter.

We're squeezed into a miniature pew. Boxes of tissues are on view.
The few front rows are roped off in blue for the family
The place is filled with the sad tide of a darkly dressed procession
of familiar faces. Some standing washed up round the walls.
Two conspicuous strangers shudder and shake with showy sobs
She's a buxom Essex blonde. He wears a check short-sleeved shirt

Are they professional mourners hired to warm up the audience?
They loudly lead the lamentation but disappear before the wake.
A crescendo of crying accompanies the cardboard coffin carried in
by faithful friends, followed by the family stumbling broken hearted
its surface of painted grass and skies adorned with daisies and butterflie
incongruous in the tangible miasma of misery uniting the mourners

They play the music that he loved to hear. Everyone sheds hot tears
His father starts to speak but the music is relentless
a chorus of keening continues when he speaks, helpless with sadness
his wife and daughter wailing while the wind howls outside
all the congregation is now crying with and for the family
except for baby blue-eyed Albert, smiling for our future

A Sonnet for Sam

Not longer striding up against the stream
The west wind, now with him, fills his sails
And sends him swiftly drifting to his dream –
The distant sapphire shores, where nightingales
Sing serenades to welcome their new boy.
Delivered from the dangers of the dark
His spirit soars into the light with joy
Supported by the sweet song of the lark.
By peaceful river he will be at ease
Eternally – learning the language of
The birds, the fish, the flowers and the trees,
The sun, the moon and shining stars above.
His torments and his troubles now are past
He's broken free and found his peace at last

Substitution

I can't get no – substitution
I'm convinced there's no solution
Coz I'm bad, yes I'm bad!
Well – I never really had a dad
And I still want what I never had

I guessed that it would end in tears
But still spent twenty seven years
Looking for the perfect chap
To fill my aching daddy gap...
My love life was a load of crap

And then – I found the perfect man –
A fellow artist, name of Dan
Not quite a dirty low-down bum
At last! I thought, my prince had come
But what he wanted was ..... a mum!

Divorced with dogs and grown-up kids
My so-called sex life on the skids
I knew no-one would want to shag
What I'd become – a sad old bag.
At least I still enjoyed a fag

No dad, no rock'n'roll – no joke!
My last resort went up in smoke
When cigarettes became taboo
Whatever was a girl to do?
My lovely roll-ups were non-U

How much worse could my life get?...
They haven't outlawed chocolate yet!
So I completely lost the plot
Bought a big bar... and scoffed the lot
And now my figure's gone to pot...
So what!

OTHER ANIMALS

Bertie Bulldog's Bargain Basement

We flog high-class clogs for puppies and dogs
Soft slippers and flippers for foppish frogs
Pinstriped and zoot suits for tadpoles and newts
Wellington boots for fastidious coots
Pillbox hats with veils for naff nightingales
And top hats and tails for in-the-swim whales

We sell flat caps and flash spats to clothes-conscious cats
Panama hats for hip pipistrelle bats
We have hipster flares for streetwise hares
Fishnet brassieres for chilled polar bears
Two-tone golfing shoes for hip-hop kangaroos
And tartan trews for punk cockatoos

We stock Argyll socks for the fashionable fox
Afternoon frocks for the tea-dancing ox
Net petticoats for line-dancing stoats
Chic camel coats for miniature goats
Espadrilles with rope soles for voguish voles
And mohair wool stoles for a-la-mode moles

We supply old school ties for posh butterflies
And snazzy bow ties for sad dragonflies
Well-cut dungarees for young chimpanzees
And cosy bootees for sharp wasps and bees
Camouflage pants for smart soldier ants
Even Y front pants for cold cormorants

Come inside! One size fits all! Every creature, great and small –
We've got exactly what you need. Your satisfaction's guaranteed!

Collared Dove

Valentine's Day: the collared doves cooing
That was the day they started their wooing
Two soft feathered fruits in café au lait
Together in winter's bare branches all day
They wove love's garlands into the night
Gently lifting my heart and bringing delight

But now one sits silent and all alone
The love of his life so cruelly gone
He still waits patiently – but in vain
Hoping that she'll come cooing again
In his tiny brain is a muddled blur
He can't quite remember what happened to her

Through my garden window only last week
I saw nature red in talon and beak
A magnificent sparrowhawk grasping its prey
Tearing at flesh and feathers of grey
Its eagle eye darting all around
While it held the dead lovebird down on the ground

The grey turned scarlet as it ripped her apart
Breaking her mate's and my human heart
Then it noticed me watching it pecking its prey
And clutching the limp corpse, flew up and away
A sad drift of feathers was all that was left
And one dove and me, both feeling bereft

Clothes Maketh Man

There he was just a walking down the street
Short fat and bald, socks and crocs on his feet
With his earrings and tattoos he really looked crap
He covered his bald head with a reversed baseball cap

 Hawaiian shirt with sunsets and palm trees
Camouflage cargo pants, two pink pudgy knees
Safari waistcoat hanging open wide
Still couldn't hide the bulging beer belly inside

Fag in one hand, beer can in the other
I reckon all his clothes had been chosen by his mother
Who'd said to her sixty-seven year old son
"For God's sake go out my boy and have yourself some fun

And while you are at it there's something you can do
Take my dear little doggy out to walk with you"
"Oh but Mum – won't I look like a bloody stupid twit
Holding a pink lead with a poodle fixed to it!"

Spyder / Midnight Rambler

Spyder! Spyder! Creeping light
In the bathrooms of the night
Who invited you to call
And terrify me in the hall?
I heard you scuttling on the stair
Suspected you'd been hiding there
An all-pervading sense of doom
Came with you into my bedroom

Why the eight legs? Why eight eyes?
And why such an enormous size?
You and I were all alone
And there was no-one I could phone
I'd have to do the deed myself!
Grabbed a glass from bathroom shelf
I could hardy bear to look
As I lifted you on that slim book

I knew you meant to do me harm
Suppose you ran right up my arm?
Already partially undressed
Barefoot in only pants and vest
Breathless, my heart missed a beat
As I ran screaming in the street
In dark graveyard I set you free
And prayed you'd stay away from me

GETTING ON A BIT

Angry Old Women Inc.

We're a miserable lot – us grumpy old shrews
We always complain about crippling shoes
We don't like the fashions – maternity smocks?
We can't stand the sight of your sandals with socks
We think natural fibres are bloody fantastic
We hate polyester, polythene, plastic
So why ever on earth are the makers unable
To use silk or cotton for a non-itchy label?

We want food to be wholesome, want our bread to be brown
We want to shop local and not out of town
We want things to be simple – so do us a favour
Forget plastic wrapping – it ruins the flavour!
When watching the telly, we tut at the grammar
Or when people say "like" or say "er", "um" or stammer
We don't go online to get all our info
We look in a book or listen to radio

We think it's outrageous to spend council tax
On spraying weedkiller on pavements and cracks
Or murdering trees – just to show off their power
One council's weed is this woman's wild flower
We like to see gardens of plants, trees and grass
You can stick your paved car spaces right up your arse
We haven't gone metric, we can't think in metres
We prefer our dimensions in inches and feeters

Our miniscule pension's a national disgrace!
We're amazed the prime minister dare show his face
Our society's riddled with so many ills
Unemployment, bad housing, extortionate bills
Quite frankly, we thought that they had to be joking
When they insisted we all stub out smoking
No sex, no drugs, no rock'n'roll for us
Only a pass for free rides on the bus

Chance Encounter in the Chazzer or A Near Sex Experience

In the Age Concern shop my heart came to a stop
As he stood there, he looked so exciting
While we talked by the books he gave lingering looks
At my lips that he thought were inviting

I was elated, excited – my pilot light ignited
I felt I was walking on air
My spirits took flight, reached a dangerous height
So I told myself to take care

Was I being a fool, was I losing my cool?
Was it just my imagination?
With my heart running riot, I kept it all quiet
I thought of my self-preservation

With a lump in my throat, I dropped him a note
Saying poetry? What do you think?
Next day when he called I was thrilled and enthralled
He was going to come round for a drink!

We sat by the fire aflame with desire
I remembered just what I'd been missing
I longed for his touch; it was all far too much
To resist – so we ended up kissing

But I thought: "I'm too old!" Turned him out in the cold
Without a roll in the hay
I was all in a tizzy, mixed up and dizzy
Could still smell the booze the next day

Don't Know What to Wear

Now that I'm older, grey in my hair
Don't know what to wear
Couldn't get away with wearing mini skirts
High heels, low cut sexy tee shirts
If I wore a clingy gold lame dress
Mutton dressed as lamb
Would I be too tarty to go to your party?
Would you give a damn?

Should I wear cardies, sensible shoes
Tweedy pleated skirt?
Should I wear big knickers like the other old girls
Twinset and a nice row of pearls?
Wearing my favourite old pair of jeans
Gives me teenage kicks
Is it imprudent to dress like a student
Now I'm sixty six?

My Bathroom or Lavatory Humour

My bathroom is out on the pavement
There's nowhere that I can pee
The outside lav's grotty so I'll use my old potty
And cut down on coffee and tea

My lavatory's out on the pavement
There's nowhere that I can crap
My life is a bummer, I need a good plumber
All I've got is one beastly cold tap

My wash basin's out on the pavement
The shower is on the front path
If there was any water I probably oughtta
Indulge in an alfresco bath

My boiler is out on the pavement
My extremities are turning blue
As I said to young Fanny, I'd sell my own granny
To see steam coming out of my flue

Everything's out on the pavement
Progress is painfully slow
I feel so dejected, I'm all disconnected
I'm messed up with nowhere to go

But who is this out on the pavement?
It's Sam with his ample white van!
He wields his great spanner in confident manner
The prince of perfection in man!

My Least Favourite Things

Macdonald's French fries and fast food in boxes
Torn pork pie packaging pissed on by foxes
Crisps full of flavours and salt – never plain
Sausage rolls rotting and mouldy with rain
Tubes of Pringles
Processed singles
Wrappers chucked around
I despair as I survey these horrible things
Littered all over the ground

Bright plastic bottles of cola and soda
Beer bottles oozing a stale boozy odour
Squashed cardboard packets without any fags
Shredded and soaking torn paper bags
Kinder bueno
Minty Aero
Chocolate multipacks
Do teenagers eat only horrible things
Salty and sugary snacks?

Zooming In and Out

She changed trains at a strange unknown station
she hoped coffee would quickly be found
as she approached her desired destination
she took a good look all around
her eyes panned across the entire scene
in a desperate search for caffeine
When she spotted the distant coffee shop
her spirits were raised more than somewhat
the hot paper cup had a loose top
but it would still hit the right spot
her next train said the big departures screen
would leave from platform seventeen

but here she was stuck on platform one
no time for a pee or a fag
to make it she'd just have to run
so she shoved the hot cup in her bag
soaking and scalded and in pain
she ran coffee stained for her train

REMEMBERING

The Bus Ride to Bath

We went on a bus ride from Bristol to Bath
My mother, my brother and me
We didn't know where we were going
Or why.
We'd never been there before.
We called it a coach, not a bus
It sounded sort of posh to us
But it was dark and dismal,
Itchy stuff on the seats
All we could see were ashtrays
Stuffed with cigarette ends
Overflowing on the backs of the seats in front
It was smoky and stinking with mud on the floor
Windows steamed up and sprayed with mud
We couldn't see where we were going
The bus suddenly stopped on the outskirts of town
And she bustled us off there
In a suburban street of terraced cottages
All the same – two up two down
We didn't think that much of Bath
So far.

We'd never been there before
But still – it was an outing
She dragged us up a garden path
And fiercely rapped on the cottage door
A pretty lady stepped out on the path
Our mother surprised us by shouting:
"I'm Mrs Robinson, Robbie's wife
Leave him alone if you value your life!"
Whack!
She smacked her round the head.
She marched back down the path again
Forgot about us and stepped on a bus
Leaving us standing in the rain
My brother ran after and jumped on too
I stood paralysed wanting the loo
Then in the distance I saw them returning
She striding, he running and crying:
"You didn't mind that you left her behind!
We didn't know where you were going!"
She gripped my arm and marched us off
My brother and I both crying
Trying to keep up in our big wellies

Going Downhill

They're walking downhill to the beach
on a seaside holiday
but you'd think that they were refugees
trying to get away
She dare not look at him or speak
nobody can smile
She tries to cover up her guilt
forever in denial

They're walking downhill together
but a thousand miles apart
that determined look he's wearing
hides his broken heart
Her parents' shadows cross their path
they're always close at hand
to protect her from the husband
that they could never stand

Mrs Robinson

And here's to you, Mrs Robinson
Pour yourself another lonely drink
Do you think, Mrs Robinson
I haven't seen the booze beneath the sink?

Fifty empty brandy bottles with the mice under the stairs
Fifty per cent proof secrets of your youth
Thirty seven sherry bottles drunk to drown your cares
Mother's ruin will swill away the truth.

You never knew, Mrs Robinson
Exactly who on earth you tried to be
Artificial accent, artificial smile
Artificial flowers on your TV.

Junk Mail

This is the last time I'm coming this way
On dangerous roads in the rain
To clear out your house now that you've gone away
And you'll never come back here again

I park in a puddle outside your front door
Fraying sandbags have spilled out their guts
I am scratched by the rose that you'll deadhead no more
That obscures your house name: 2 The Butts

The letter box gapes with obsolete mail
The door ploughs through a postage tsunami
Catalogue cataracts crying out for a sale
And appeals from the Salvation Army

I kick it aside and can now close the door
And survey the dispiriting view
There is only one handwritten card on the floor
From someone that I never knew

I look round for somewhere to stack all this stuff
But each surface is covered with crap
Five cloths on the table – more than enough
Underneath there's a fleece and on top – bubblewrap

The Living Room

The first thing I could see as I crept in the room
Was the greenish glow of the telly through the gloom
Where granny was drinking a nice port and lemon.
The TV evangelist was shouting about heaven

He'd woken me up – I'd been in bed since eight
And this programme was broadcast remarkably late.
I'd never heard anything like it before
Being just nine in nineteen fifty four

All was presented in stark black and white
Giving me, at that age, an almighty fright.
What was this about? I didn't understand
I noticed the Radio Times close at hand

And saw the headline: "The End is Nigh!"
While Bill Graham ranted: "You're going to die!"
"Oh No! Even Me? Oh Blimey!" I thought
And my granny gave me a nice drop of port

He kept on talking about the "Good News"
Which, to my little mind, befuddled with booze
Was depressing, disturbing and much more like Bad
I wasn't ready to abandon the short life I'd had

Reluctantly I went back up to my bed
Where I stared up at the stars instead
Looking heavenward made me feel rather small
And I tried hard to imagine the Nothing at All

That I'd find if I flew to the end of the stars
Beyond Jupiter, Pluto. Neptune and Mars
And still, as I drunkenly dropped off to sleep
I prayed to the Lord my soul for to keep